The Church: Oh Dear

By David F Pennant

David F. Pennant
3.12.24

Silver Lining Books

Woking

1

The Church: Oh Dear

copyright © David F Pennant 2024

ISBN 978-1-7392029-5-8

Bible translations are by the author

Published by Silver Lining Books

30 Oriental Road, Woking, Surrey, GU22 7AW

www.pennantpublishing.co.uk

Contents

The Church: Oh Dear

"To uproot and to tear down, to destroy and to overthrow, to build and to plant."

The calling of Jeremiah the prophet

One – Finding Faith

When I was in my mid teens, it was time to get confirmed in the Church of England, I thought to myself. The other boys in my boarding school house tended to do it, and I had always been brought up in the Church of England, so it seemed a sensible course of action.

The weekly talks in preparation were more interesting than I had expected them to be. I found myself enjoying them to my surprise. This was in contrast to my experience of services in the school chapel, which I had found dull. There had been a time when on a hymn being announced, I would note how many verses there were in it and mark the half way point in my mind. Then when we had sung our way to that place, at least there was the satisfaction of knowing that we were half way through that particular hymn. My strategy helped make the hymns feel more bearable. Frankly, a service in chapel was an endurance test.

Then there was the occasional point of interest to be noticed from the names of the hymn writers, printed above the words of the hymn. F. A. G. Ousley (1825 – 1889) – was he perhaps a heavy smoker, I wondered? And J. Ellerton (1826 – 1893) who was also long dead – were there jelly babies around in his time? I thought probably not. Life was tough in those days, I knew.

I can recall just one sermon from my school days. The preacher was worked up about 'Xmas'. "Put Christ back into Christmas," he urged us boys. It seemed like a good idea to me at the time, but I wasn't sure what it meant in practice.

Arising from all this religion, I once decided I was going to be a good person, and the way to do it was to pinch myself hard on the thigh every time I slipped into bad behaviour. This attempt at self-discipline only lasted thirty-six hours; my thigh was getting so painful from all the bruising. I felt alarmed; was it really so hard to live well? I soon forgot about the experiment and just carried on with my duties.

The classes came to an end, and the confirmation was to take place on a Sunday in November. On the Friday before there was a day of preparation. We all went in a coach to a chapel in London. I discovered that the plan was to spend the day in silence, meditating. This struck me as particularly unwelcome. Still, as with so much else in my life in that time, the thing to do was to grit my teeth and submit to what my elders and betters had planned for me.

There were to be four talks interspersed with the silence, given by a visiting clergyman. The first one brought me up short.

"You boys mean nothing by this," he began. "You will attend communion for three weeks, and after that you'll forget about it and never go again probably. You're wasting everyone's time."

Cheeky so and so, I bristled. I felt incensed. I forget the rest of the talk.

Then it was time to sit on an upright chair in a cheerless room and think of... what? It all seemed interminably long to me.

I noticed that every now and then, a boy would get up from his chair and leave the room only to return a few minutes later. What was that about, I wondered? Finally I grasped that they were visiting the loo. I can be very slow at times.

I had a brainwave. I would get up and go out too – nobody seemed to ask any questions when the other boys did so, but instead of visiting the loo I would go into the empty chapel. I wasn't going to stand for this wasting everybody's time nonsense.

I entered the chapel, which was deserted, looked at the altar with its small cross standing on the top, and said in a firm voice, "I give my heart to God."

Straight away I sensed that God was present, there in the chapel with me, and that he was pleased with what I had just said. My offer was accepted. It was a revelation.

As I returned to my seat in the other room, I reflected that there was a God after all and that he was interested in me and I could know him. I decided then and there to do find out what he wanted me to do and be.

We returned to school. The Sunday of the confirmation soon came. The bishop would lay his hands on my head at the climax of the service, I was told, asking God to fill me with his Holy Spirit. The other boys getting confirmed were busy wondering what would happen at that moment. When it came to my turn to be done, I sensed nothing at all. Never mind.

My friend Stephen discovered somehow that I was a 'born again Christian' as he put it – I felt rather alarmed by this idea, and he dragged me along to the school Christian meeting which happened once a week after lunch on Sundays. It was only half an hour long, which was bearable. There would be a different visiting speaker each week.

A member of staff used to give me Bible reading notes, which I neglected. However, in the end I got started on them, and worked my way through John's Gospel, using a booklet containing daily readings with a paragraph of comment by somebody. There was a scene showing a fine sunrise on the front cover, with a family in silhouette walking towards it, which I rather liked. It gave a sense of being on a journey into the light. I went through the booklet three times in a row over the course of several months.

When I arrived at university, I joined the Christian Union and finally decided that I agreed with what people had told me often enough, that the Bible was the word of God. I began to get to know it and study it.

All this was to ink over what I had written in pencil that day in the chapel in London. What I hadn't realised at the time was that in making my decision, I had unwittingly joined the church, which is made up of believers in Jesus. It's time to consider that now.

Two – Joining the Church

So what exactly is the church? Or rather, what did Jesus want his church to be? This may seem a tedious question to some readers but I assure you, a careful examination of the key Bible texts is critical. Please bear with me.

I take it as a given that the authority on this matter is to be found in the Bible text. There is only one Jesus, and that's the one we read about in the gospels. I hope you can accept that.

To set the scene, let's start with some words of Paul in his letter to the believers at Ephesus which gave me a helpful overview. He wrote,

"It is by grace we are saved..."

We are saved by God's kindness towards us. Lovely news. One church I belonged to for a while read no further than this; everything was grace in their eyes. But the sentence does not stop there. There is more to it than that.

Let's press on in.

"It is by grace we are saved, through faith..."

Now we see that the grace of God only becomes ours when we believe in it and accept it. It's like click and collect; the item may be yours, fully paid for, but it's not in your hands until you go to the collection point and take possession of it.

I realised over the next few years that, as Paul put it in his letter to the Romans, "All sinned and fall short of the glory of God" (including me, as I well knew). "Death is the payment for sin, but the gift of God is eternal life through Jesus Christ our Lord." I needed to thank God that although I deserved the death of a sinner, I was forgiven because of Christ dying on the cross in my place, and I needed to accept God's gift of new life personally. This is what I did. This was to make the grace of God my own.

But there was still more to come in Paul's words to the Ephesians.

"It is by grace we are saved, through faith, and this is not of yourselves; it is a gift of God, not of works, so that no person might boast. For we are his creation, created in Jesus Christ for good works which God has prepared in advance so that we might walk in them."

This was important. I could not earn my way into God's good books by my good works (ha-ha, the very idea) but now that I had accepted my new life by faith in Christ, there was a job waiting for me to do.

That's what the church is; the company of believers in Jesus doing the good works we have been called to do.

Think of the army. "Right," yells the sergeant major to the men standing on parade in their smart battle dress, "I want four volunteers; Smith, Roberts, Jones and Evans. You four, fall OUT. About TURN. Form a column (shuffle, shuffle). By the left, quick MARCH" or whatever army drill is these days. My days in the school corps are long gone.

Volunteers or conscripts? Difficult to tell. I had given my heart to God but now I had joined up there was something expected from me.

Let's look at what Jesus said he wanted his church to do and be.

It turns out that he only mentioned the word *ekklesia*, which we translate 'church', on two occasions. From the book of Acts, we learn that the *ekklesia* was the town council, in other words, a group of people with responsibility for their area. *Ek* means 'out' and *klesia* is from a word meaning 'to call', so we grasp that the church is the group of people called out from the crowd to do a task. Like our local councillors today in effect.

On one occasion when he used the word church, Jesus said that if there was a problem between two believers and a few people acting together could not sort it out, then they should "take it to the church" as a last resort. From this we grasp that a church is composed of a number of believers acting together.

The other thing he said about the church, when talking to Peter, was "on this rock (Greek *petra*) I will build my church, and the gates of Hades (hell) will not win a victory over it."

Exactly how Peter was foundational to the church has been the subject of debate, but what I want to point out is the character of the church as revealed in Jesus' words. It is to overcome the gates of hell. I have a mental image of a battering ram breaking down a strong gate so that the prisoners can escape. The church's job is to be a team releasing people from hell by forcing the gate open. It won't be easy; imagine the arrows flying thickly and boiling oil being poured down from the ramparts. Wonderful but frightening. Better have your armour on, as Paul put it to the church at Ephesus – belt of truth, breastplate of integrity, gospel shoes, helmet of salvation and sword of faith.

The final text I want to refer to is Jesus' words on departure, as they add further points of direction. They come at the end of Matthew's gospel.

"Jesus said, 'All authority in heaven and earth has been given to me. Going out, then, disciple all the nations, baptising them in the name of father, son and Holy Spirit, and teaching them to keep all I have commanded you...'"

The good work the church is to do is to bring the nations to follow Jesus. Believers are to go through baptism, and be taught to do what Jesus had taught his followers to do.

His words conclude with a promise: "...and behold I am with you all days until the completion of the age." That's good. We have Jesus' help in our task.

So to summarise, the church exists where believers in Jesus are acting together with him to make all nations his followers, baptising them, releasing people from hell and teaching them to follow the instructions he gave to the twelve.

I used to admire the work of the German evangelist Rheinhard Bonnke, who would share the gospel with people in Africa in large meetings. His team used to have a huge tent for holding the gatherings, until it got destroyed by the elements during a storm, so after that they gave up on tents and met in the open air.

I recall excited speculation as to when there would be a million people present at one time in a meeting. In the event, it was thought there were one million six hundred thousand at a meeting at Lagos in the year two thousand.

Reinhardt wrote two books about his work. The first was called *Plundering Hell*. That's not a bad summary of Jesus' prediction about his church destroying the gate of hell. A few years later, he wrote a sequel and called it *Populating Heaven*. That's a pithy way of expressing the final words of Jesus, so could we agree that if the church needs a strap line, and everybody seems to want a strap line these days, then it might be 'The Church - plundering hell and populating heaven'.

I now discover Rheinhard wrote a book later on called *Hell Empty – Heaven Full*. Right on target. Great stuff.

When I signed on the dotted line, I was joining the company of believers involved in this global rescue plan.

Now, with these thoughts in mind, let's see how well the twenty-four churches I have attended over seventy years have actually done.

Three – Twenty-four Churches Considered

I say twenty-four churches, but that includes chapels at my two boarding schools and university. Most of the rest were Church of England churches, but there were also Baptist and unaffiliated churches too. I have also attended 'high' church services often enough to get the idea. In all, I have experienced a reasonable cross section of Christian life in our nation.

Two of the churches were ones that I led – poorly, I now consider. I would do things very differently if I had another chance today.

Could any of the churches be described as plundering hell and populating heaven? I'm afraid not. Most of them did what we did in the two churches I led, where the focus was on Sunday morning worship, including Bible teaching, prayer, singing, and celebration of Holy Communion (sometimes called the Lord's Supper). There were also home groups and appropriate meetings and occasional special events on week nights. Some years there would be a church house party or a week's visit to a summer Christian conference. Not much of a sense of rescue from hell in any of that.

Did Jesus ask his followers to do the things we did? Let's examine them briefly one by one.

We'll start with gathering together to worship. It has come as a shock to me to realise that Jesus never raised the subject of worship with his disciples. He appears to have had no interest in it. What about teaching the Bible which I used to do? No, he never asked his followers for that. Prayer together must have a place, surely; praying was something he did a great deal. True, but he did not ask us to copy his lifestyle; he insisted that we teach what he commanded the twelve, and that did not include the kind of group praying we did.

What about singing together? Alright, we read that at the end of the Last Supper, "when they had sung a hymn, they went out to the Mount of Olives."

Phew, thank goodness for that. Singing is in then.

Well no, it's only something Jesus did, not something he asked his followers to do. It's also good to get singing in proportion. The phrase in Mark's gospel should probably be hyphenated, when-they-had-sung-a-hymn, as it is just a single word in the Greek (*umnesantes*). I find it impossible to render it as one word in English – 'hymn-sung' is the closest I can get.

It's a throw away remark and nowhere near as central to their lives as we make it today. Consider this. Jesus healed and delivered thousands of people from sickness and demonic oppression and sang one hymn. Over the course of my Christian life I have sung and accompanied around twenty-five thousand hymns and songs (I play piano and organ) and attempted to heal and deliver only a few hundred people. Note the contrast. I've had things back to front.

Holy Communion? Well, if you read the accounts of the last supper carefully, Jesus gave them bread and wine, yes, but the impression given in the gospels is that it was a one off. You have to look at Paul's first letter to the Corinthians for the idea that this should be repeated.

What about the home groups, meetings and times away? These tended to more of what we did on Sundays for the most part. I have also been associated with churches which used to run courses on marriage or bereavement or the like, but Jesus never asked his followers to do any of that either.

I grew up with these practices and accepted them without thought as an expression of church life, but now I have had time to reflect on them, I realise that they never came from Jesus himself.

We have somehow managed to turn the new way of living that Jesus brought into a religion. I suspect that when non-Christian people in our country hear the word church, they think of a sturdily built building which stands locked for most of the week except for Sundays when a few people enter for a church service. The idea that these people are meant to be God's shock troops called to plunder hell and populate heaven never crosses their minds, any more than, if we are honest, it tends to cross our minds.

By now some readers will be hopping up and down. How dare I denigrate worship? And Bible teaching? And Holy Communion? And gatherings for prayer?

We need to examine each of these practices in detail over the next few chapters and, if possible, determine why it is that we regard them as indispensible ingredients of church life and are so attached to them. Then, if you agree with me that we need to make amends, we will be ready to consider how we might do church better in future. To build and to plant, to quote Jeremiah.

We will take these four customs in reverse order – prayer, communion, Bible teaching and then worship. Much of this material may be difficult to accept for most readers because of what we are used to. I ask you not to be too hasty in throwing my presentation overboard but to remember where we began, which is that the church has a job to do in plundering hell and populating heaven by obeying Jesus' commands. My question is, how can we become that church more closely?

A thought before we begin. Jesus warned us that false messiahs would come after him and lead people astray. The question is, am I one of them, seriously misguided, and in danger of misleading people? Or as I suspect, have we been led into ways opposite from what Jesus intended by a whole series of false messiahs, of wolves in sheep's clothing? Jesus and Paul predicted there would be many such people coming after them.

What do wolves in sheep's clothing look like, we ask ourselves? Well the answer is that they look like sheep. Not easy to detect, therefore.

Paul wanted the Christians at Corinth, when they prophesied one by one – I imagine a circle of about twenty people, to examine and test what was said. This is your role from here on as you read my arguments. Please have your antennae up.

Four – Prayer

Praying together has been a key part of the churches I have attended.

I used to be very keen on long hours spent in prayer. I remember berating a meeting of the college Christian Union on one occasion when I was the student in charge of it. If A W Tozer could spend five hours each morning stretched full out on the shore of Lake Michigan in prayer and worship, then so should we, I urged.

I sincerely hope now that they took no notice. Our question needs to be, what did Jesus say to his followers about prayer?

The answer is not much. It was the twelve who raised the subject rather than him, when they said "Lord, teach us to pray."

He replied with the so-called Lord's prayer, "When you pray, say 'Our Father in heaven, may your name be holy, may your will be done on earth as it is in heaven, give us food for today, forgive us our wrongdoing as we forgive others, don't put us to the test and deliver us from evil'."

That was it. The first thing I notice is how short it was. Indeed, he introduced his teaching by telling them not to be long-winded in prayer. Keep it simple.

In an attempt to obey his commands more closely, as we discussed earlier, I have limited my early morning praying to the Lord's prayer for some months now. I do also briefly remind the Lord about half a dozen of my friends who are going through it – A who is physically sick each morning over the state of his finances, B whose insides are in a shocking state, C whose Parkinson's is robbing him of mobility and now hearing and whose wife is in a home with severe dementia, and a few others in dire need. I hope the Lord doesn't mind. I regard it as more in line with his practice to be a friend to them and visit them and pray with them in person than to pray for them at a distance.

That feels more like the stories of Jesus in the gospels who dealt with the individuals in front of him.

In the churches I have been involved with, we have tended to pray together about wars and conflicts overseas, perhaps pray for the church leaders, maybe remember the monarch and parliament in a nod to St Paul who asked that this be done, and pray that God would heal sick people who are not present.

Jesus never modelled any of this, and we don't see it in the book of Acts either. Indeed, I realise that we asked God to heal the sick, but actually, Jesus asks us to heal the sick. We had it completely back to front.

Jesus' idea of prayer was to maintain constant communication with his father in heaven. Even during the day when he was surrounded by crowds he would 'only ever do what he saw the father doing'. Prayer for a sick person was a word of command in their presence not a request to God carried out at a distance. There was plenty of conflict in the world of his day, but he never prayed about any of it to our knowledge.

Ah, but we have a healing group in our church that lays hands on the sick.

That's good to hear. But be careful. In the churches of my experience, what that has meant in practice is there being two or three people available for prayer ministry at the end of the Sunday morning service. It's an add-on which most church people ignore. Maybe just one or two percent of the church people are actively involved in this. Outsiders have no idea that this takes place.

People are apt to claim that such a church has a healing ministry. Well, I'm not impressed myself. Don't claim your church has a healing ministry until every member is involved and practising it all week, to my mind. I have even witnessed elderly people in such churches get sicker and sicker and then die without ever going near the ones offering healing prayer. Whatever is going on? It's such a long way from Jesus and the twelve.

Still a miniscule healing ministry is closer to Jesus' commands than no healing ministry at all. We must not despise the day of small things. Perhaps it can grow.

Jesus did offer a number of one liners to help us with our individual prayer lives which are revealing. On one occasion he told the people the story of the unjust judge to encourage them to persist with prayer and not give up. This implies that God may not answer our prayers at first hearing. He wants to see if we keep at it, to know if we really mean what we ask.

Another time, when the disciples could not cast out an unclean spirit, Jesus explained that this kind could only come out through prayer. This makes prayer sound like a tool to be used. Interesting.

On the night of Jesus' betrayal, his followers were to watch and pray lest they be caught out. It's good to pray before a testing time or a tricky assignment.

Prayer would move mountains if it was done the right way, he said – with faith in God, or as the Greek allows, holding onto the faithfulness of God. Once again the feeling of prayer as a tool for a purpose.

Finally, there was an occasion when Jesus was moved by the wretched state of the crowds. They were like sheep without a shepherd, as he put it. Or like a crop that was now ripe and needed harvesting. He told the twelve to 'ask the Lord to thrust out labourers into his harvest'.

Here is one of the commands Jesus gave the twelve, and therefore one we are to seize on as well, as we saw. Let's use it as a test case. How well have my churches done regarding it?

I have been watching for years, and none of my twenty-four churches have ever prayed on a Sunday morning when I was present that God would raise up people into Christian work of this kind. Why ever not, when Jesus asked us to pray for it specifically? Are we so slow to grasp what he wants?

I find the whole area of prayer challenging myself, and you may feel my emphasis is wrong, but nights of prayer, meetings for prayer, prayers on Sunday mornings in the service all fall outside what Jesus instructed the twelve and hence us to my mind.

If these things were done in addition to obeying the commands of Jesus, that would be one thing, but in practice, as with a number of the other church habits we are going to inspect, they are done instead of obeying Jesus. They are therefore an unhelpful distraction in my opinion.

One moment. One hundred and twenty disciples prayed together leading up to the day of Pentecost, and later on, when Peter was in prison, they gathered to pray for him.

True. This raises the question as to how our practice today is to be shaped by what the early church did. We will consider this towards the end of the book. Please hold on to that thought for now.

As regards the gathering of the hundred and twenty, I once heard a preacher claim that the Holy Spirit came because of the prayer meeting, but this is to misread scripture; he came because Jesus had promised that he was coming soon. He would still have come if the disciples had been playing snooker to my mind, but this would have been difficult as the game was not invented in those days. Never mind.

Part of me found that paragraph hard to write. Isn't it irreverent of me to be talking about snooker in the same sentence as the

Holy Spirit? Where's my sense of holiness and awe?

Since my earliest days, I have been taught reverence. When I went to the local church as part of a primary school outing, there were urgent disapproving whispers all round me from the other children as we arrived lest I enter God's building with my school cap still on. I soon whipped it off, and have remembered the incident to this day. I was to recall where I was. No messing around in the church.

With my adult hat on, I now ask where all this supposed reverence came from. I suppose the answer is from the Lord descending on Sinai in a way which inspired trembling in the people, and from the days of Jeremiah when God described his word as a consuming fire and as a hammer which breaks the rock in pieces. What did those two sets of people have in common? They were taking God and his requirements lightly, pretty much ignoring him. They needed to be brought to their senses.

But does that mean that there is an ongoing call on us to cower in God's presence? I don't think so. Jesus went out of his way to describe God as our heavenly father who wants the best for us. So to my mind it's unfortunate that our cathedrals seem to call for silence, for the atmosphere of the academic library. Any talk of holy buildings is unhelpful to my mind, as it's half way to turning the joy and simplicity of following Jesus into a religion. Please can we get away from that?

As regards the meeting later on in Acts when the united believers gathered together to pray for Peter, note that it was for a specific purpose, intense, focused and in a response to peril. Our prayers in the service on a Sunday morning tended to be the opposite to be frank.

In contrast to us, I'm reminded of the time when James Hudson Taylor, the pioneer missionary, was calculating how many mission stations would be needed to cover a vast area of inland China in the nineteenth century. He realised that nigh on seventy extra workers would be needed. He then remembered the passage about Jesus sending out seventy others. Was this what the Lord had in mind? A fresh seventy for a fresh age?

He decided it was. So he prayed a definite prayer for the coming seventy, marking the day in his diary. But he did not stop there, with a vague aspiration. He soon had all the other missionaries under his care praying the same thing in unity, and he started to make preparations for the workers who would come. The large expansion of the mission he now expected called for a number of changes. Finally, he made plans to return to the UK – the sea trip would last many weeks, to receive the seventy new recruits and then bring them out with him to China. His faith, prayer and actions were in tune with each other.

The prayer was duly answered and the seventy arrived. Note the feeling of prayer as doing business with God. It is in line with John's words in his first letter about prayer: "This is the boldness we have towards him, that if we ask according to his will, he hears us. And if we know that he hears us, whatever we ask, we know that we have the things asked for, which we have asked from him."

If you are keen to pray together, then before you start, get the whole church to agree together about what the will of God is for you at this time, a process which might take some months or even years, and then when everyone is agreed and on board, by all means offer united, persistent, urgent prayer about it.

I hardly need to add that none of the churches I have been in have done anything like this. What we prayed for on Sunday mornings week by week was pretty much haphazard. We missed the point.

This observation is turning out to be a repetitive refrain.

Five – Bread and Wine

Believers have shared bread and wine together in memory of Jesus since the year dot. Blood has been shed over differing interpretations of what is meant by the custom, tragically. What a terrible mistake it was to have got so worked up over it.

Let's look closely at the origin of the practice.

Jesus and the twelve were celebrating the Passover upstairs in the annual meal. By giving them the bread and wine as his body and blood at this moment, Jesus was saying to the disciples that all the animal sacrifices of former times were now fulfilled in his death. That's how I understand it. It explains why we don't bring bulls and lambs along to be slaughtered at a temple as the Jews did any longer.

It was Paul who reported his words 'do this as often as you drink it', as we mentioned before. Did he mean every time you have a meal together?

Paul's letter to the Corinthians implies that the people of those days made it a frequent event. There's also a case for saying it should be done once a year as a replacement of the Passover meal, to my mind. 'As often as you drink it' could have the sense of as often as you celebrate the Passover.

One thing I am clear about; the sharing of bread and wine was to take place during a meal.

What have we done in practice?

Well, we have taken away the meal for one thing and replaced it with an hour of liturgy in the case of the Church of England. Jesus never asked his followers to do that. Worse, all kinds of traditions have sprung up around it. To give an example, I was once prevented from receiving the bread and wine in a church I visited because I had not attended confession two days before. Thanks a lot. That notion does not come from Jesus.

When I was a church leader, as curate in charge (without hyphens), the archdeacon told me on one occasion that a service of Holy Communion was not valid unless it contained collect, epistle and gospel. The collect was the special prayer, and the epistle and gospel were the Bible readings for that Sunday. At the time I felt chastened by these words from my superior. I clearly needed to get a grip.

Now I regard the statement as being without foundation as it has no connection with Jesus at all. It reminds me of words in Peter's first letter telling church leaders not to behave like 'little tin gods', in J. B. Phillips' translation. In laying down the law, the archdeacon was behaving as if he was God in this instance. Who was he to say what he did?

It's very easy to misuse authority in this kind of way. I once came across an A4 printed sheet of instructions for Rural Deans from a Bishop lying on a desk in a church office. A Rural Dean is one below an archdeacon, and has oversight of a number of parishes. There were a dozen numbered paragraphs on the sheet.

Instead of reading it straight away, I turned the sheet over and asked myself what I would have chosen to be number one, the most important matter for the Rural Dean to attend to.

What about 'Encourage all your people to seek first the Kingdom of God in love for all, especially for enemies' or something similar, I thought to myself.

Then I turned the sheet over, and read number one. 'Any instance of a lay person celebrating Holy Communion is to be reported to the Bishop immediately.' Oh dear. Is that really what matters?

I used to hate the idea that I was the one person allowed to 'celebrate' and that everyone else's role in the service was to watch. How could I do something to lessen the impact of this, I wondered?

I decided that I did not need to stand by the bread and wine for the rules to be satisfied; it would be okay as long as I said the required words anywhere in the building. I chose to position myself twenty metres away from the 'holy table' (what on earth is one of those?) among the rows of the worshippers and speak out from there. Too bad that I hadn't the courage to get everyone present to join in the words too. Then it really would have been the body of Christ – the assembly, instigating the body of Christ – the elements, for the body of Christ – the people again. Or so I thought at the time. Now I regard the whole thing as so much nonsense. Sorry if that offends you, but we seem to be a mile away from Jesus and his friends sharing a meal together.

Nobody commented on my adopted practice. They probably did not grasp what I was doing and barely noticed.

Talking of behaving like little tin gods, it proved remarkably easy even for me to do it. Let me explain. I was told that as curate in charge of a daughter church without hyphens in my title, I had no authority. This seemed disappointing.

"What would I have needed to get hyphens, to become curate-in-charge?"

"Oh, the bishop would have had to lay hands on you or something similar."

"What would the difference be if I had the hyphens?" I persisted?

"Oh, then you would still have had virtually no authority."

I thought to myself that I would have preferred to have virtually no authority than no authority at all, but never mind. The thing to notice was the contrast with Jesus, who had all authority in heaven and on earth, as we read earlier. Obeying him was what mattered. Why should anybody obey me?

Anyway, the day came when there were to be weekly confirmation classes at the mother church, the kind of thing I had gone through at the start of my Christian journey. I announced the opportunity to the people during the service.

At the end, a person with brain damage and consequently some awkwardness in behaviour came to me and said they would like to attend the classes. My immediate reaction was that their presence would affect the group negatively, so I said that I thought it would not be a good idea and to leave it be. Arranging lifts to get to the meetings was going to be difficult I maintained. The person was very disappointed.

As I turned away, a thought formed clearly in my mind, 'that's oppression'. I barely knew what oppression was in those days, but I was dimly aware it was something bad. I somehow managed to swing back round and say, "on second thoughts, I think we can do it. I'll ask around to see if someone can collect you and take you along each week." The person's relief was marked.

I soon found another church member who wanted to attend the classes who was happy to take a passenger in their car each week, and the confirmation took place in due course with the candidate I had tried to dissuade included.

This story makes me look bad, which is just as it should be as that is what I am, but the point of telling it is for us to notice how easy it is to act abusively in the role of leader. We won't build church like that. A sure way of getting the Holy Spirit to leave. May God preserve church leaders from being the stopper in the bottle by their attitudes and actions. It's easily done.

No meal, a lot of man-made rules and regulations, only certain people allowed to 'celebrate' – it's all a far cry from Jesus' simple instructions about bread and wine to the twelve at the Passover meal. So sad. And did he even want the activity to take centre stage as it does in so many of our churches? Shouldn't it be something incidental as it was in his own case? Didn't the time and effort we devoted to it when I was curate in charge deflect us from the main task of making all nations disciples?

Six – Bible Teaching

When I finally had the chance to lead a church, I used to enjoy preaching. I worked my way through Philippians and other biblical books on Sunday mornings, including Daniel and Revelation as I recall.

Why did I do that? Well this was what preachers did in the tradition I came from. The Bible is the word of God and teaching it to the people was the thing to do.

It was only recently that I reflected that Jesus himself never asked his followers to teach the Bible. He did not do it himself, either.

There was just one occasion on the road to Emmaus when he explained the things in the scriptures concerning himself to two disheartened disciples after he had risen from the dead. Not that we learn anything about the prophecies from it; Luke's gospel does not give us any hint of the content of that talk.

Jesus had a high regard for the scriptures, quoting them frequently, and on one occasion saying to the Sadducees, "You are deceived not knowing the scriptures and the power of God." When he was dying on the cross, his words "My God, my God why have you forsaken me?" were a quotation from the opening verse of Psalm twenty-two, which contains a graphic description of the horrors of crucifixion. According to John, he was also aware of the need for the scriptures to be fulfilled when he said on the cross, "I thirst."

So Jesus lived and breathed the Scriptures, but when it came to addressing the people, he used to talk to them in parables. Indeed, he never spoke to them without a parable.

So why didn't I and my elders and betters whom I admired speak in parables and choose to go in for Bible exposition instead? It's strange when you think about it.

Actually, Jesus did lay down a teaching programme, as we saw earlier. His followers are to "teach them all I have commanded you (the twelve)."

I only grasped the significance of this after I had left church leadership, which I did for personal reasons that are not relevant to our task. So by now I was sitting in the pew listening to others speak on Sundays.

I decided to conduct a survey to see how often the subject of a talk was a command of Jesus to the twelve.

The result was a revelation. Out of the following one hundred and eighty talks – that's about three and a half years' worth of sermons, just two were on commands of Jesus. So disappointing. I stopped counting in the end – it was too depressing.

What I have never heard stated from the front is something along these lines.

"Good morning everybody. Now for the foreseeable future, we are going to be looking at the commands of Jesus on Sunday mornings. This is because of what he said at the end of his time with us on earth. Turn to Matthew chapter twenty-eight and verse twenty, and you will see that followers of Jesus are called to teach the commands of Jesus to believers that come..."

This may be a good moment to consider the delicious fruit cake that my wife taught me to make. Cream together 226 grams of unsalted butter and 226 grams of Demerara sugar, then stir in three eggs, adding them one at a time. Pour in 283 grams of self-raising flour along with the fruit, which is 452 grams of sultanas and a 250 gram pot of glace cherries, fold it all together gently, put the mixture in a non-stick tin which I also line with grease-proof paper, and cook it for one hour in a pre-heated oven at 180 degrees and then for another half hour at 150 degrees. Test it with a knife to check it is cooked all through, turn it out onto a wire rack and you have a fine fruit cake every time.

I even won second prize with this fruit cake in the bake-off at Woking's Lighthouse a year or so back, but there were admittedly only five entries so don't let's get too excited about it.

One day I discovered that this cake is known as Winston Churchill fruit cake. Interesting. Then a while later, I read in a biography of Churchill that there was a fruit cake he particularly enjoyed which he called Bismarck Cake. So I reckon my fruit cake tradition goes back as least as far as Bismarck. Perhaps it was the kind of thing Marie Antoinette had in mind when she made her remark about the poor people eating cake. Who knows?

So with regard to the tradition of teaching the Bible on Sundays, I know it goes back to the previous generation, but my guess is it probably stretches back to Calvin preaching in Geneva in the 1500s and maybe beyond.

I have much admiration for godly leaders from the past, but when push comes to shove, I want to follow Jesus the Messiah and not be deflected by traditions that have grown up, no matter how good they appear to be.

Considering the cake again, imagine replacing the cherries with a tin of sweet corn. Please don't try this at home; for one thing, the result might taste disgusting. But my question is, could I still call it Winston Churchill Cake if I did that? I don't think so. It would need a new name.

I have an even more horrid thought. If I was to replace the sultanas with gravel, could I still call the resulting mixture a cake? How much say do I have regarding the ingredients?

Please keep this thought about tampering with instructions in mind as we continue our enquiry.

But the Bible is so important.

Agreed, and knowing it well seems to be in line with Jesus. Paul's knowledge of the Hebrew Bible never ceases to impress me, and have you noticed that his entire argument in the letter to the Romans is all based on a tiny throwaway remark in Habakkuk? When reading that so-called minor prophet (once again, life can be tough) if you blink you have missed it. Also, Paul often draws inferences from passages in the Hebrew Bible which I barely knew even existed.

How are we going to know what the commands of Jesus are if we don't read the Bible? And how can we use it as a toolbox unless we have the tools at our finger tips?

Ninety-five percent of what I know about the Bible has come to me through reading it over and over again and memorising verses from it. As someone once said, the best commentary on Scripture is Scripture; I seldom find the need to look at Bible reading aids these days. Paul once said, "We possess the mind of Christ," and if we want to possess it too then becoming familiar with the text seems key.

But that does not mean teaching it in a gathering, to my mind. Rather it is something I can do at home. I recall a new convert once saying to a group of us, "I read Luke on Thursday and Acts the day before. What shall I read today?" Better than any number of sermons, I reckon.

For those who find reading hard and prefer to listen, there are free audio recordings of the Bible online.

I'm beginning to wonder whether the mistake we have made in churches has been to do things when gathered together which would be better done by individuals at home.

Let's see if that thought gains traction as we proceed.

Finally, do you realise that it is possible to reduce the complete package of Christian teaching to just one sentence? Let's give it its own page to make it stand out. When you are ready, take a deep breath and then read on...

Do everything that Jesus commanded the twelve.

There. You don't actually need any more teaching now you have read that. It's simply a case of establishing what Jesus told them, which you can do on your own.

Notice how brief and simple it is, like the Lord's Prayer. Anybody can grasp it.

Seven – Worship

Jesus did not raise the subject of worship with his disciples, therefore it does not fall within his commands to his followers, therefore the church is mistaken in gathering together in order to worship.

Thank you for reading this far. The idea that the church is first and foremost a worshipping community has been drummed into us from the cradle, so I expect to lose most readers at this point, but some will be prepared to hear me out, hopefully. Please hold on and read further before binning the book.

Just to be clear, the Church of England starts its Sunday services with the words from the front, "We have gathered here in order to worship God..." I have taken part in such events between five and ten thousand times by now. It's deeply ingrained in our culture, with around fifty thousand well-established buildings dedicated to the purpose, many of them with a spire like a finger pointing upwards towards God. The word church is synonymous with the phrase 'worshipping community' in our minds.

In my opinion, gathered worship is a distraction from what Jesus wanted his church to do and to be. It's an act of disobedience to my mind.

But Jesus told us to worship God in Spirit and in truth.

Let's look at some of the relevant passages in the Bible which seem to contradict what I have said at first hearing.

We need to be careful to note who said what to whom here. The story comes in John's gospel chapter four.

The Samaritan woman is feeling uncomfortable because Jesus knows that she is now with her sixth man, and he is not her husband, so in order to deflect the conversation she asks why Jews gather to worship in Jerusalem but her ancestors worshipped on this mountain. In his reply Jesus said that it's not the place but the manner in which you worship that counts. Those that worship God should worship him in spirit and in truth.

Jesus was not speaking to the disciples but to one woman. This is not a general appeal to the church to gather for worship, when you think about it. Rather, Jesus is saying, if there is to be any worship, it must be carried out by people whose lives are right. What was the good of this lady's worship to God when her love-life was offensive to what God had lain down?

Regarding the arguments over bread and wine which we considered earlier, it's a shame that the people did not notice verse seven of chapter one of Zephaniah's little book, another minor prophet, which reads, "When God calls a sacrifice, he sanctifies the worshippers who are present." It's the people in the meeting who need to be made holy, not the elements. The same thought applies here too with regard to worshippers.

There's a picture that relates to this in the prophecy of Zechariah. Joshua the priest is standing before the altar, but he is seen to be dressed in filthy robes. These need to be attended to before he can proceed.

So too with our gatherings for worship – what is the state of the people? How can people so committed to ignoring God and doing things their own way as we are be described as worshipping God in spirit and in truth?

Please note that Jesus did not raise the subject of worship; it was the woman. Worship was not an interest of his. However, it so happens that in this very passage, his heart's desire was revealed.

When the disciples returned from the village where they had been buying food, shortly after the conversation with the woman, they urged Jesus to eat something.

"I have food to eat of which you know nothing," he replied. "It is meat and drink for me to do God's will until I have finished his work."

That's where his heart lay, and it's where our heart should lie too. What does God want me to do, us to do? Once we know, let's do it.

I have heard several appeals about the importance of worship based on the first part of this passage, that we are to worship God in spirit and in truth, but not one of those speakers has mentioned the verse about Jesus' food and drink that comes further down the page. I find such presentations unbalanced.

This thought brings us back to our main theme. How can we say we are interested in doing God's will if we are ignoring the commands of Jesus? And what is the use of what we call worshipping God in this case?

Paul said we were to sing Psalms, hymns and spiritual songs to one another.

This comes in his letter to the Ephesians, with a similar passage in the letter to the Colossians. Actually, there is a poor translation here. Greek *eautois* means 'to yourselves' rather than 'to one another'. The Greek for 'to one another' is *allelois* which Paul happens to use a verse or two later on. So the verse would be better rendered, "speaking to yourselves with Psalms, hymns and odes, singing and psalming to the Lord in your hearts."

This verse does imply worshipping God in song but it does not mention gathering together for the purpose. I imagine it might mean that while we are going about our daily life, we have worship songs in the back of our minds, as we would say, or in our hearts as Paul says. Humming them over. Or these days, maybe playing them on a portable device.

I remember hearing about a man with a demonic problem who filled his home with praise songs all hours at a considerable volume. One day he heard a voice in his head say "we're leaving", and he found that he was now freed from his trouble. There's a fine use for all this godly music that we now have.

Once again, worship seems to be for individual use rather than in the gathering.

But the Psalms are full of worship and they were Israel's hymnbook.

Wrong on both counts, I'm afraid. There are exhortations to worship in the Psalms, most memorably in number one hundred and fifty, but the majority of the material in the Psalms does not fall into the category of sung worship. Psalm one hundred and five was sung at the dedication of Solomon's temple, true, but that is the only instance we read of group singing I can recall. There is no other mention of community singing anywhere in the biblical story of Israel from the creation to the exile. Apart from anything else, the sound of any singing at the temple would have been drowned out by the braying of all the animals being slaughtered. It is vain to imagine that the singing in our weekly assemblies reflects a practice stretching back to the year dot. Read Leviticus to see what actually went on, or rather what was meant to go on, because there is very little evidence that it happened in practice. It seems they were no better at obedience than we are.

What about the synagogues?

What about them? I suppose you mean that it was Jesus' custom to go to the synagogue each week and we are carrying on the tradition by our worship services.

There's actually no instruction in the Hebrew Bible about synagogues or a weekly meeting. The practice grew up when the Jews were in exile, as a way of keeping the faith alive. The word synagogue means a 'gathering together', from *syn* or *sun* 'together' and *ago* 'gather'. A good idea for an ex-patriot community that wants to maintain its identity.

So what you are saying is that because the weekly gathering existed in Jesus' day and he attended, we should continue the tradition in our churches.

Not that we make any effort to find out what happened in the synagogue meetings back then. I don't have the first idea, beyond hearing once that men and women used to sit separately, and I have never witnessed that practice in our churches. I don't think we make the slightest effort to copy synagogue life.

It's also interesting to note that we only know about his attendances at synagogue because of the remarkable things that happened there – a withered arm healed here, a demonised man set free there, the murderous uprising in Jesus' home town synagogue on another occasion.

Fundamentally, your suggestion is that we should do what Jesus did. We will examine this idea in due course.

It was while Paul and Barnabas were worshipping the Lord at Antioch that the Holy Spirit sent them out on their mission.

Worshipping the Lord and fasting, actually, but most of us aren't keen on fasting these days so we tend to overlook that detail. Why be accurate and precise when handling scripture? Why not bend the text to suit our taste? Overlooking something in the text that we don't like – does that sound familiar?

So your point is that it was when they were deeply involved in worshipping and fasting together that they heard the voice of God most clearly and that worshipping and fasting together is therefore the thing to do.

I suppose the finest talk I ever heard was on this very subject. It was given by Alan Redpath to the Cambridge Christian Union on a Saturday evening in the Union debating chamber in the early 1970s. It made a lasting impression on me. I can even remember where I was sitting in relation to the speaker; I was a number of rows back, and I had a clear view of him because of the arrangement of the seating. By the time he had finished, I had a huge sense of the importance of worshipping together accompanied by fasting – I disliked the fasting bit and soon forgot about it, but I was committed to the worshipping part.

When I was finally in charge of a church of my own and we gathered on Sunday mornings, I used to find that it took forty minutes or so before the people were warmed up. By the end of the service we had a good worshipful atmosphere going.

This was difficult. Having to work hard to energise our meetings felt like the strenuous effort my father used to have to make to start our Wolsey car in the 1950s by turning the crank handle. Thank goodness someone invented the self-starter.

I found myself reflecting on the problem of making a cup of tea near the North Pole. Imagine the scene. Once the small gas ring was alight, the kettle would be placed on it, but the water left over from the previous occasion had frozen solid, so even getting it liquid took a long time. Then the water had to heat on up to boiling point despite the intense cold – it was sound practice to shield the kettle with our bodies from any wind that was blowing. Finally the glorious moment would arrive when the kettle began to whistle. The water would be poured out quickly onto the tea bags in our cold tin mugs – mind my fingers please, and why had nobody thought to warm the mugs? Cold milk was added. By this time the brew was at best lukewarm but no matter, the thing to do was to swallow it down promptly with a pretence of satisfaction and appear to enjoy the experience.

That was how our weekly worship felt to me much of the time.

I had a brain wave. What if the band was already in action so that when the people arrived they would enter to a glorious sound of worship in progress? Keep the kettle boiling, as we used to say when we were small children jumping on and off a pile of hay in turn outside the farm next door to where I used to live.

Our small church lacked facilities, but I reckoned that in a town or city, the Christians could gather enough bands together to keep the worship songs flowing continually. At Las Vegas in America, the casinos never close day or night and gambling is continuous; couldn't we manage to have perpetual praise? Then people could come in as they were able and join in for as long or short as they wanted.

I became excited about this idea, and we tried it out. We managed to have continuous worship from three in the afternoon until ten at night one Sunday, despite being only sixty strong. People came and went at will.

We only ever attempted it once – there was no call for a repeat.

I used to imagine continuous worship taking place in an inner city. Perhaps it could be my next job. As you can see, I was as keen on gathering for worship as anybody in those days.

Then one morning, as I was thinking about it in our bedroom, I found myself imagining a tramp coming in to an otherwise empty church building while a band was playing, to keep warm. This seemed troubling for a moment, but then I thought, why ever not. Let anybody come in who wants to.

It was about that time that a member of the church rang me one Thursday morning.

"David, we must do stuff for the homeless."

I groaned inwardly but kept my cool. "Well done, Jane," I replied. "Go on telling us what God is saying to us about homeless people."

We wrestled with this issue for another eighteen months before I found myself standing up one Sunday morning saying that I believed God wanted us to keep our church building open in the coming winter for rough sleepers who had nowhere to go.

The response was that everyone looked the other way until the idea fell flat on its face as it was bound to do.

This provoked a crisis for me. The believers had all been happy with the idea that we were to find out the will of God and do it until their pastor stood up with a proposal that was unwelcome. They were not even willing to discuss it with me.

What was the good of our so-called worship on Sunday mornings if our hearts were so unwilling to respond to God's call, or even to something which might or might not be God's call, that the leader proposed?

Perhaps I had misheard or had been deluded in what I had said to them, but would it not have been the right thing to have told me so?

Small wonder that my enthusiasm for gathered worship took a knock.

Eight – Hearing God's Voice

This seems to be the right place to discuss my experience of hearing from God. We will get back to Acts chapter thirteen after that, I promise.

The story about the brain-damaged believer that I told earlier involved a clear thought entering my mind, which is something I experience occasionally. More often, words that I hear from God are less insistent than that – an impulse to make a phone call, or the thought that maybe it would be good to contact X or Y. I also get pictures that come to me. But there has been one occasion when I heard God's voice loud and clear inside my head as an audible voice.

It had happened a few years before during my first post as a clergyman when I was assistant curate. The church was holding a week of outreach meetings, and we had been invited into the local secondary school to address the Christian group there. It was an open meeting, a chance to share the gospel.

A friend of mine in the church was speaking very ably from the front, and I was sitting in the back row behind two dozen teenagers. I was disappointed not to be doing the talk myself – I would love to have explained the good news to the group. Why do I never get the chance to share the gospel, I thought to myself.

The meeting came to an end and we all went our separate ways. I was the last to leave, and as I was walking out of the school, I had to pass through the school hall. I entered by one door, and as I did so, a member of staff entered by another door aiming for the same exit as myself, and we found ourselves walking shoulder to shoulder. It was a most strange situation.

The thought formed in my mind, talk to this man about his soul.

I knew what that meant. I had previously read and been impressed by a biography of the nineteenth century American evangelist D. L. Moody, whose practice was never to let a day pass without talking to someone about their soul, as he put it. There had been one night when it got to ten o' clock and he realised he had not talked to anybody about their soul that day, so he hurried outside and found someone under the gas lamp in the street and had a conversation with them about faith in Christ.

I had been impressed and convicted about this. I find starting up a conversation about following Jesus with an individual very hard, although I am more than happy to address a public meeting on the subject. In fact the rowdier the better; I once happily faced a baying mob of teenagers at a youth club on a Friday evening who were hurling abusive comments about Jesus at me, that he was a pervert etc.

Oh dear, I thought while walking along beside the stranger with the words 'talk to the man about his soul' in my mind. I'm going to pretend I did not hear that.

We reached the exit and our ways parted. He went to the right, I to the left. That was when I heard the voice. It was inside my head and as clear as a bell.

"When are you going to start obeying me?"

It was deserved. I had been rebellious. What's the matter with me? Why was I so opposed? But *start* obeying God? Hadn't I been doing that for years? Hadn't I got ordained into his church?

I felt really bad for a few days. The shame of that event has never left me, and to be honest, I'm not looking forward to the day of judgement when I will have to look God in the eye. I have been so weak in trying to follow my Lord.

I'm no good at personal evangelism even now, but I have made a little progress. Paul advised the Colossian Christians to study how best to talk to each person they met.

I've found that humour is a help. I recently joined a long slow-moving queue in an eatery at a popular National Trust property one lunch time. There was a single man behind me about my age, so to start a conversation I said "Do you think there will be queues like this in heaven? Because if so, won't that turn it into hell?"

He turned out to be a Christian man, as did the couple in front of us in the queue, and we had a pleasing conversation which helped pass the time. Maybe I will summon up the courage to ask a stranger about their attitude to Jesus one day. I hope so. Why am I so timid?

I don't think I am alone in my reticence. The last time someone stopped me on the street to ask me if I believed in Jesus was on

Poole Hill near central Bournemouth about fifty years ago. In fact that is the only time it's happened to me during my lifetime that I remember.

Other outreach efforts I've encountered in public? I recall a church band bringing worship songs onto the street in our town a few times, but not within the last fifteen years. My reaction at the time was, why worship songs? It seemed a strange choice to me.

From my experience I would say that we Christians have lost our public voice and retreated into our ghettoes over time. Then we wonder why not many churches are flourishing.

Back to Acts chapter thirteen, when Paul and Barnabas heard from God and responded.

It only struck me recently that Alan Redpath had expounded the word 'while' in that passage as if it meant 'as a result of'. He was really speaking as if the text says "As a result of them worshipping and fasting, the Holy Spirit spoke..." His understanding was that worshipping and fasting drew them into God's presence in a way that allowed them to be more sensitive to the prompting of the Holy Spirit than they might have been otherwise.

There is however another possibility. What if Paul and Barnabas already knew before the meeting that they were called to go out on mission but had allowed themselves to get distracted into worship and fasting instead? In that instance, the Holy Spirit was urging them to get on with what they knew they had to do.

Read the sentence again carefully, and you will see what I mean about the two possible ways of taking it:

"While they were worshipping the Lord and fasting, the Holy Spirit said 'send out Paul and Barnabas on the mission to which I have called them'. So they laid hands on them and sent them off."

In my opinion, the words 'to which I have called them' makes it sound more that the latter possibility was the case rather than the former. Paul and Barnabas were finding it hard to get started.

Here's an interesting thing. We read "While Jesus was walking beside the Sea of Galilee," he called two fishermen to follow him. It would never occur to us to understand that as "As a result of Jesus walking beside the Sea of Galilee," he called two fishermen to follow him. But we are inclined to read the 'while' in Acts chapter thirteen in that manner. Why might that be?

I suggest we have all been so firmly brainwashed by the frequently repeated idea that worshipping God together is the key activity of the church that we see it even where it is not present.

Gathered worship seems to be a universal instinct. All over the world we witness numerous religions, with their temples and shrines and holy places and worshippers. We have behaved as if Jesus came to usher in a religion like them when, in my view, there is no solid evidence that he did. Indeed, we noted where his heart lay earlier. It was in the obedience to his father's will that I failed at so spectacularly when I was challenged to reach out to the stranger.

I use the word brain-washed deliberately. I have thought about this subject for years. It's taken me a long time to become sure about what I am saying. I believe that all our cathedrals and churches and worshipping traditions have been misguided. Gathered worship is not what believers are called to do. I believe we have been deceived.

A final thought about Alan Redpath's talk. The key point of the verse is that Paul and Barnabas were called to go off on a journey of outreach, but Alan did not speak about that. The talk was all focused on the importance of worship.

That's a little strange if you think about it. We only know that they were worshipping and fasting at Antioch because the Holy Spirit called them to a task at that time. Their devotions were incidental to the call of God.

I'm puzzled about our tendency to make worship the be all and end all of church life. I find it odd.

Nine – Meeting Together

Doesn't it say that we are to meet together?

Yes it does, but rather than assuming that this is a call to gather to worship, let's turn to Hebrews chapter ten and see exactly what it says. I offer a wooden translation.

"Let us consider one another (Greek *allelous*) into a paroxysm (*paraxusmos*) of love and good works, not leaving off synagoguing (*episunagogen*) ourselves up, as some do, but entreating, and this the more so as you see the day approaching."

Interestingly, the Greek words for 'one another' and 'synagogue' which we discussed earlier both make an appearance here as you can see.

Note that the purpose of the meeting is not to worship but for everyone to stir each other up to love and good works. I love the use of the Greek word from which we get our word paroxysm, which only occurs twice in the New Testament. Fun.

My experience of church meetings is that they are led by one or at most two or three people, and all we others are expected to sit quietly on seats during the meeting. All of us stirring each other up to love and good works is precisely what doesn't happen at such events.

Since I gained this insight about the importance of mutual stirring, my policy has been to arrive at church half an hour early and talk to people as they come in. Then I put up with the formal event, until there is another chance of talking with people afterwards. Sometimes worthwhile conversations happen, and then I feel good about having attended. On other occasions, sharing together is not so easy and I go home disappointed.

Recently I went to a Sunday morning service scheduled to start at 1030. I was the first person to arrive, at 0950. A handful of people came in gradually from ten onwards, but at 1020 the place was so empty that I decided things were finally falling apart for this congregation. However, I need not have worried. The people all flooded in to take their seats between 1028 and 1032 and the meeting began. Then at the end, a good proportion of them hurried out, off to their ovens set on timers containing their Sunday lunches I expect. If you want that attitude expressed theologically, I suppose one might say the favourite doctrine of those souls was roastpotatoesification. Encouraging each other was not important to them.

Here's a curious thing. When I was a boy, my parents had friends called Robin and Benny with whom they played bridge regularly. They were delightful people. Robin's shoes were always polished spotlessly, as my father often pointed out to me, hoping I would pick up the habit of shoe polishing as a result, and Robin also collected stamps. He kindly filled some gaps in my collection one time, when he had reached the fine old age of one hundred and one.

I had always assumed that Robin and Benny were non-believers, but I discovered by accident one day that they attended the same church as us. We always arrived in good time for the service and sat near the front, while they came in at the last moment, sat near the back, and were first out of the door at the end, so I never saw them there. This went on for about eight years. Extraordinary.

Small wonder that some churches only have the quality of fellowship as is found between strangers at a motorway service station, as I once heard it put. How am I even to learn people's names, I ask myself, something I find hard enough when meeting someone new at the best of times. It's as if they don't want to be known.

This contrasts markedly with an evening in Woking many years ago when Pastor Bob was over from California. It was a large gathering on a Saturday evening as I recall.

Bob was called forward later on in the meeting. He stood quietly at the front, and then said gently, "There's a woman wearing a purple coat near the back – would you be willing to stand, please?"

The lady stood.

"I think you have been to the doctor recently," Bob continued. She nodded. "And had difficult news." Yes again. "I believe you were told that you have cancer." Once again a nod.

"Well, the Lord wants us all to pray for you." We did so accordingly.

"Now there's another lady two or three rows from the back – would you please stand?" A young lady did so. "I believe you got married recently?" Yes. "In fact, I believe that is your husband working the sound system at the back of the meeting." It was so.

"And I think you are hoping to start a family" Bob went on. "Yes," she acknowledged. "Well this is to say that the baby is on its way."

The lady sank down in delight and confusion.

All this was new to me. Is this really God or some sort of scam, I wondered? I reckoned that if it was from God, then it meant that we were to go in for a very much deeper level of fellowship and sharing in our churches than I had ever witnessed.

I decided I had better meet Bob at the end of the meeting if I could, to try and find out what was going on. When things broke up, I went towards the front as others were leaving, and there was a chance to speak to Bob. I introduced myself.

We were soon talking about something when in the middle of what he was saying he added, "And you will be hanging on by the edge."

I gulped. In the previous twenty-four hours, two images had come into my head at different times. One was of the back of a Mini car with fingers of two hands clinging onto it as if someone was trying to escape from inside the boot. The second was of a church pulpit, with just the two hands visible of someone trying to hang on to it from the front.

This stranger was interpreting my pictures to me without knowing what they were. It was like Daniel explaining the meaning of king Nebuchadnezzar's dream to him without having been told what the dream was about.

I don't know what happened to the lady in the purple coat, but I did see the baby that was born to the newlyweds nine months later.

The prophecy about me would also come true over the following few years; I will never forget hammering with my fist on the carpet in our bedroom one morning begging God to end my life, a scene which recurred periodically for about twenty months until it finally passed. It was a very difficult time. God doesn't always answer prayer in the way we would like, please note. He had warned me about the coming difficulties in advance, through Bob, although at the time I had not taken much notice to be honest, and I failed to draw comfort from the words at the time of my distress. Only later did I manage to see things in perspective, that God was with me even in my darkest days, and that it would enable me to comfort others going through hard times in due course. Make medicine out of poison, as the saying goes.

Some of us may have been feeling nervous and unprepared for battering ram service in the kingdom of God. I hope some of these stories about hearing from God and him being in charge will remind us that anything God has asked us to do he will also enable. We are not sent into battle without equipment. We have our toolbox – the Bible, targeted prayer and the Holy Spirit with his presence and gifts.

I hope you feel I have made adequate answers to the various objections to my stance on meeting for gathered worship that were drawn from the Bible. Just to recap, these were

But Jesus told us to worship God in Spirit and in truth.

Paul said we were to sing Psalms, hymns and spiritual songs to one another.

But the Psalms are full of worship and they were Israel's hymnbook.

It was while Paul and Barnabas were worshipping the Lord at Antioch that the Holy Spirit sent them out on their mission.

The first objection relates to Jesus himself, and therefore has the potential to carry the most weight to my mind. The other three, along with any more arguments in favour of gathered worship that may occur to you, are drawn from elsewhere in the Bible.

To attempt to qualify Jesus' clear instruction about what we are to do, made in the light of his having all authority in heaven and earth, seems mistaken to me. Texts from the old testament and the rest of the new testament should not be misused in this way.

Because of Jesus' statement that believers are to obey what he taught the twelve, I want to be part of a church that obeys those instructions, the whole of those instructions, and nothing but those instructions.

I have known the Spirit of God to be powerfully present in a meeting whose purpose was worship.

So have I. One of the churches I attended had a remarkable season of that kind. I could not bear to miss a week. It was most exciting. There was much laying on of hands and answered prayer for all sorts of conditions and situations for weeks on end. I could feel the Holy Spirit's presence in the meetings in a remarkable way.

Then one week, I found on arrival that nearly half the people present were wearing red badges indicating that they were the ones assigned to offer prayer. I felt unhappy about this development, instinctively, not just because there was no red badge for me. Then a week or two later the badges disappeared and it was announced that the elders were the ones to offer prayer. Before long, anyone who wanted prayer was to go to the pastor, and soon after that, we did not hear about prayer of that kind at all.

I sensed that the Holy Spirit had left our meetings some while earlier. Had we driven him off by trying to control and channel the flow of the river of fire, turning it into a canal that suited us? But then this always had been a church where there was a considerable degree of control exercised from the top.

I simply had to recognise that the Spirit or wind of God blows where he wills, as John put it in chapter three of his gospel, and he had chosen to blow into our meetings and then out again. I did not know what to make of it.

Jesus once promised that where two or three believers met in his name, he would be there in the midst. This being so, I find myself wondering why it is so often the case that I can attend church on a Sunday morning and, to be frank, not really sense the presence of God in the meeting at all.

I think the reason may lie in the words 'in my name'. When we gather with the aim of worshipping God but ignoring the call to be the battering ram that breaks down the gate of hell and the evangelists that populate heaven, we put Jesus in an awkward position, since we are not really meeting in his name at all. If he turns up by his Spirit, then people will think it is because of the worship, but if he does not, that seems a bit mean when there are all these believers present who are trying to honour God as best they know how.

Surely God would not leave us in ignorance about gathered worship for centuries, which he has done if what you say is right.

Please don't be too sure about this. Consider this example.

Jerome translated the Bible into Latin in the late fourth century. The translation came to be known as the Vulgate. It was pretty much the only Bible text to be used in Europe until Greek scholars arrived from the sack of Constantinople in 1453, eleven hundred years later, and the original Greek text was rediscovered.

Jerome's translation of Mark chapter one verse fifteen ran as follows. "Jesus came into Galilee... and said... 'the Kingdom of heaven is at hand; do penance and believe in the good news'."

When the original Greek text came to be studied, they found the sense was different: "The kingdom of heaven is at hand; repent, and believe in the good news."

Penance is an action, rather like a forfeit, but repentance is a change of mind or outlook. The two are quite different.

Think of all the godly souls doing acts of penance century after century, thinking that they were pleasing the Lord by their deeds. God was prepared to allow that state of affairs to continue for a millennium, even though it was misguided, so it seems reasonable to me that he would also have allowed the church to continue as gathered worshippers who left obedience to Jesus' commands to one side all this time even though it wasn't what he wanted.

Can't we do both worship and outreach?

It seems not. I have been in several churches where there is an occasional move to do outreach. It lasts for a week or two, and then we go on as we did before. Trying to do both won't work in practice.

Also, why add disobedience to obedience? This runs the risk of repeating the awful tragedy and trauma of the book of Leviticus, chapter ten.

In the opening chapters of Leviticus, God gave Moses precise and clear instructions as to how the sacrificial system was to be run. It was to be overseen by Aaron and his descendents. However, the day came when two of Aaron's sons Nadab and Abihu thought they would add an offering of their own. The name Nadab actually means 'volunteer'.

They offered unauthorised incense burnt in censors, and paid for it with their lives on the spot. They were snuffed out, and Aaron was even told by God not to grieve for them. As his boys, they were to have been in charge of the whole sacrificial system.

The message was very clear indeed — don't mess around with God's instructions. For something similar in the era of the early church, read the story of how Ananias and Sapphira came to grief in Acts chapter five. Their problem was dishonesty before God and the church, pretending to be one thing when they were another.

Jesus did not call his followers to plunder hell and populate heaven for fun, on a take it or leave it basis. Those with a casual attitude who feel able to play fast and loose with his words should remember the warning of James, the Lord's brother; "Don't let there be many teachers, my brothers, seeing that we will receive a greater judgement."

I think we are finally in a position to sum things up. Worship is the attitude of believers, but we have made it the activity of the assembly. The activity of the church is to carry out the programme that Jesus laid on the twelve, and the purpose of the assembly is to enable that to happen.

As we obey the commands, we will in fact be expressing our worship by our actions, probably without realising it. John wrote in chapter five of his first letter, "For this is the love of God, that we keep his commands."

Worth pondering.

Ten – Now What?

So what should a church look and be like?

I have struggled with this question for some years. I find it hard to visualise the kind of church I am describing when it doesn't yet exist, as far as I know.

I want to give this matter some serious thought. Let's start by citing some examples of best practice that I have witnessed.

When I lived in Bristol, there was a church called Pip and Jay – I think it was St. Philip and St. Jacob really, which was known for one thing. They were focused on raising money for Christian work overseas.

Before going near the place I grasped that if I chose to attend a service there, it was not a matter of whether I would make a donation to the cause – it was a question of how much it would be. It would be no good trying to hold back, either. I needed to get my wallet out properly or not attend at all.

When I finally entered the building one Sunday evening, the first thing I saw was a large notice giving the total amount of money raised so far that year. It was well into six figures, and clearly represented a great deal of sacrificial giving considering the size of the gathering.

My reason for mentioning this is that here was a church that was known all over Bristol for standing for a particular cause. None of the other churches I have attended were known for anything in this way beyond the fact that they were churches.

I reckon the church of the future ought to be known for plundering hell and populating heaven in this kind of way. It ought to be the first thing you hear about the church.

Here's another practice I admired. I once met a young pastor of a small church in Soho,

London. He explained to me that whereas churches often have house groups, home groups, bible study groups, even life groups, their midweek groups were outreach groups. Members of those groups knew that every week, the discussion would be about how their outreach was going. There would be reporting back on their failures or successes of the week just gone, and planning ahead of future outreach efforts. I thought at the time what a great idea that was. If you were a member of that church, you were committed to outreach. Simple as that.

Here's another experience I had. When I was a student, I remember doing some door to door work with a Church Army officer in Islington, London. Some of the homes we visited were known to him, and some were cold calling. I felt nervous before we set out, but in the event I rather enjoyed it. I found that once I got started talking with people on their doorstep, the words would begin to come. It was also helpful having two of us, because while one of us was talking with the householder, the other could be marshalling his thoughts. Jesus sent out the twelve, if you remember, and also the seventy in pairs. We will think about them shortly.

I admire the Jehovah's witnesses for their door to door work. Eight or ten times I have had a visit from a pair of earnest people on my doorstep down the years. I feel sad for them that they do not acknowledge Jesus as being God as well as man; they follow Arius of early church times in that respect. Apart from everything else, they miss out on the forgiveness of sins which is only possible because of Jesus' unique status. The crucifixion was God taking on himself the consequence of the sin of the world.

So unfortunately they were not sharing the good news. We have a wonderful message to proclaim. Let's not forget it or be apologetic.

I haven't had a visit from the witnesses for some years now. Perhaps they have been put off by all the negative publicity they receive. Or maybe the little blue notices we all have by our doors now saying no to cold callers discourages them. Who knows.

Another thing I did as a young person was to organise a 'squash'. I invited fifteen friends to my parents' home one evening, gave them food and drink, and then we listened to a speaker, the Rev John Collins of Canford Magna in Dorset in this instance, who explained the Christian good news to us clearly and engagingly.

I never asked any of my friends afterwards how they had got on with the meeting, which seems barmy looking back now, but the idea was a good one.

Again as a young person I used to hand out tracts in the street. The one I liked looked like a newspaper cutting with a headline which read

Eternal News

Man Alive after Death and Burial.

It was produced by the Victory Tract Club. A splendid name. I must have given out several thousand of those tracts in north London where I was based for a time.

Then one day a traveller in a railway carriage told me he resented the intrusion, that he was pleased to get away from the demands of life when travelling home from work, and did not appreciate what I was doing. I felt chastened. At the same time an older Christian whom I admired said that the thing about tracts was that they were rather tip and run, and were perhaps not the best way of doing outreach.

I allowed myself to be put off and stopped giving out the tracts and have not done so since.

Writing this, I recall a conversation D. L. Moody the American evangelist had with a church member on one occasion. We mentioned him earlier.

"I don't like the way you do your evangelism," the man said.

"How do you do your evangelism, then?" Moody enquired.

"Oh, I don't do evangelism" the man replied.

"Well, I prefer my way of doing evangelism badly to your way of not doing it at all," Moody answered.

Point taken. Nothing we do will be perfect. As Isaiah put it, all our righteousness is as filthy rags. But the thing is to do something to make all nations Jesus' disciples, and make outreach central to church life and practice.

I feel daunted by the all nations bit.

So do I, but don't forget that this instruction to convert the whole world was given to twelve frightened men who had let Jesus down recently. Eleven actually, as Judas Iscariot had blown it. Hardly a promising outlook. I expect they felt daunted too, but they got on with it.

I recall a visiting speaker who helped inspire a group of us who were in teacher training with a view to becoming heads of music in secondary schools.

"If you aim for the stars, you might reach the moon. If you aim for the moon, you might reach the top of the lamppost, and if you aim for the top of the lamppost you might get an inch off the ground."

He then gave us a plan for getting a symphony orchestra going in a school over a five year period where there was no previous musical tradition. Great stuff.

None of my twenty-four churches had a five year plan for winning the neighbourhood to Christ let alone a plan for the world.

However, when I was appointed curate in charge, I was told several times that my predecessor but one had visited every home in the parish over eighteen months. This was discussed in my presence and was clearly much appreciated. I think people were hinting that I might copy his example.

I felt it would be much better if all the church members did the visiting, not just the minister, but I failed to organise this and I don't believe it ever happened. I focused on visiting the elderly and the sick. I think they were pleased.

I was not a good church leader, and I find it depressing to look back and reflect on how weak my attempts at outreach have been. Paul could have done the same – spent his time feeling awful about the Christians he had persecuted before he saw the light, but very sensibly his attitude was "Forgetting what is behind, I reach out to what lies ahead." Let's make efforts to copy him in that. I confess I find it very hard to do so myself; the past keeps raising its ugly head in my mind. Tiresome.

Eleven – Setting Out

Having looked at several examples of churches trying to obey Jesus in evangelism, let's now look at how he got his team going.

On the occasion when Jesus sent out the twelve, they were instructed 'to visit the places he was planning to go to'. They were to heal the sick, raise the dead, cleanse the lepers, cast out demons and preach that the kingdom of heaven had come near.

On a later occasion, he also sent out seventy disciples, in pairs. The only thing we know about them is that they were delighted when they returned because even the demons had submitted to them in Jesus' name. They were thrilled to be plundering hell.

Healing the sick has been adopted by a number of churches, but we have tended to offer it to members only, as we mentioned earlier. This does not seem right. It needs to be out there.

I note that the Jehovah's witnesses never offered to pray with me or for me when they visited. Perhaps they don't have the vision for it. I did hear of a church once that went visiting door to door asking what they could pray for on behalf of the people that lived there. Imaginative. I never heard how they got on.

However, unlike laying on hands for healing, casting out demons has not penetrated far at all into today's churches. Indeed, some dioceses in the Church of England have deliverance officers whose task is mainly to dissuade people from attempting to cast out demons. There seems to be fear around the subject.

Once I had accepted that Jesus' instructions to the twelve included healing the sick, as we saw just now, I wanted to learn to cast out demons, but I had no idea how to begin. I certainly did not want to experiment on someone who was already troubled and risk making a bad situation worse through my cack-handedness. A terrible thought.

Mind you, for all my life until that point, I had imagined that there were no demons around today. They seemed to have died out to my mind. Times had changed. Then I noticed that in the Bible, evil spirits, or unclean spirits, only ever showed up during the life of Jesus, apart from a few in the book of Acts. It's as if his presence flushed them out into the open. Maybe they are still active in people today, I wondered, but prefer to operate in secret.

How might one detect them, I considered. Jesus said the thief came only to steal, to kill and to destroy. People whose lives were being stolen from them, even destroyed, might be a place to look, I surmised.

I also noted Paul's list of fruits of the Holy Spirit – love, joy, peace, patience, kindness, goodness, faithfulness, gentleness and self-control. Characteristics the opposite of these might indicate a demonic problem, I thought. Hatred, misery, restlessness, impatience, what a horrible list was emerging. One which caught my eye was the opposite of the final fruit of the Spirit, lack of self-control. People in the grip of something they could not master. Might there be a demonic element in their suffering maybe?

I once had the chance to attend a seminar on addiction. When the opportunity came to ask questions, I raised my hand.

"Can you comment on the relationship between addiction and demonisation?" I enquired.

The speaker dodged the question and the meeting came to an end without the matter being addressed. Disappointing.

Then there was a move forward. I was sitting in a church one day during a service in which I had no active role and my mind wandered during the talk. This is a frequent occurrence for me. I wish speakers would keep things short and to the point.

My eyes strayed onto the stained glass windows. There was one of Moses holding the two tablets of the law. As I considered it, the words formed clearly in my mind, "That's demonic."

This seemed extraordinary, but I had no doubt that this thought was from God. I made some enquiries about the window, and discovered that when it had been made, installed and revealed a few decades earlier, the congregation had responded in astonishment, "Oh look, it's the vicar."

Further enquiry revealed that such a thing was a masonic practice and it turned out that many of the men in the church had been members of the local lodge of freemasons to that day. I felt troubled by this. We looked like a Christian church, but who or what were we really committed to?

It so happened that week that we had a lady to supper one evening who had formerly been a friend of my wife's. My mind was not on the event – I was too troubled by the demonic window, so I was barely listening to the conversation. Then I heard our guest was saying, "It's remarkable. She can spot demons in people as they are walking towards her."

I jerked to attention.

"I'm sorry," I apologised, "my mind was elsewhere. Who is it who has this gift?"

"My mum," came the reply.

"Right." I had clearly missed a chunk of the conversation. So rude. "Where does she live?" I enquired casually.

"In Kent." That was many miles away, but a thought occurred to me.

"Does she ever visit you?"

"Yes. She's coming up this weekend actually."

I asked if I could meet the lady, and a few days later the mum came round and we had a conversation. I told her I wanted to learn about demons, as Jesus had instructed us to cast them out.

"I've read all the books on the subject I can find, and the best one is *Christian Set Yourself Free* by Graham and Shirley Powell. In fact, my daughter told me of your interest and I've brought you a copy if you would like it."

This was excellent. I thanked her warmly. I read it over the next week.

Graham was a committed Christian who was an evangelist in New Zealand. He used to address large public meetings urging people to accept Christ. However, his personal life was not as it should have been. He suffered from sweating, restlessness and worse by day and horrible nightmares by night. Prayer only helped a little, and he found that fasting gave some relief but not much.

In the end Graham decided that he had a demon. However, despite talking to other Christian leaders in New Zealand, he couldn't find anyone who would agree with him, let alone who would attempt to cast it out. So he decided he was going to have to do it himself.

He raided the scriptures for verses that he could apply to himself. One was from Paul's first letter to the Corinthians, chapter six, where Paul wrote "Do you not know that your body is the temple of the Holy Spirit?" Another was from John's first letter, chapter one. "The blood of Jesus cleanses us from all sin."

So Graham used to spend long hours insisting, "I've given myself to God and so my body is the temple of the Holy Spirit, so get off me you horrible demon. I put myself under the blood of Jesus which cleanses me from all sin so leave me, you foul presence." He had other verses he used as well, but those are the ones that I remember.

The struggle was intense, but he insisted and persisted and after eighteen months, he was finally free.

This was wonderful. I had the answer to my problem. The way to learn how to cast out demons was to practise on myself.

As it turned out, I did not have long to wait. There came a Friday when I knew that I had to lead the music for an informal session of worship at the church on the following Tuesday. I had made so many 'mistakes' in what I had done previously in leading church services – there was a strong sense in that church of what was right and proper and my liturgical bungling was simply not acceptable, that I was terrified of getting it wrong on Tuesday. This was because I knew the songs I would like to use, but I was sure that my choices would be frowned upon severely.

I was really gripped by fear. Then I remembered Graham's book. This fear was ridiculous.

"In the name of Jesus, get off me you fear!" I declared in a forthright manner. To my great surprise and delight the fear vanished immediately, and did not return. When the event came on Tuesday, it passed off well.

So Christians could have demons after all, contrary to what I had been taught. If Christians can't have demons, then why is the last phrase of the Lord's prayer present, where we ask 'and deliver as from evil'?

I was learning how to use the Bible as a toolbox myself, a concept we mentioned earlier.

Some time later, I had a call from one of the house group leaders.

"David, there's a young man in our group that I simply cannot deal with." There followed a list of problems to make one's blood curdle.

I got to I know Phil (not his real name) and he agreed to meeting with myself and two others for prayer. We used to meet at the church in the evening once or twice a week.

In practice, it was a case of working through a whole host of issues. A theme which kept on recurring was of sin that needed confessing. We claimed the verse in John's first letter, chapter one, "If we confess our sins, God is faithful and just to forgive us our sins, and to cleanse us from all unrighteousness." Much like Graham had done. I remember laying hands on Phil and commanding spirits to leave a number of times through the weeks.

Please note that sin can include the category of bad things which have been done to us where we fall short of God's glory, not just offences we have committed. "Lord, I'm in a bad place because of ... and I'm not giving you glory in my life as a result. I confess my wrong state..." is a good way to pray, because then we can claim the forgiveness through Christ's shed blood for the area where we fall short, it seems to me. Trauma, addictions, wrong relationships and other damaging matters can all benefit from this treatment I reckon.

I also recall seeing an image of huge chains in my mind one evening while we were praying, with each link weighing perhaps a hundredweight. "I've just seen a chain," I began, and would have continued but Phil was already unclasping a tiny chain from round his neck with a small trinket hanging on it.

"It was from my grandma," he explained. "I was wondering whether it needed to go." By this stage he was keen to see the deliverance process through; he had found the praying hard to begin with, but was now appreciating the results. He wanted every trace of what was wrong out of his life.

I was mystified about the connection between his chain and my picture at the time, but now I wonder whether that little chain was weighing him down in some way, which meant that to him it was heavy, as in my thought.

The Israelites were told to have nothing to do with molten images and the like when they entered Canaan but to destroy them ruthlessly. It's easy for us to have things that drag us down in our lives today. Even Derek Prince, the respected Bible teacher, once realised that the four dragon decorations on his sitting-room wall were uncomfortably like the horrible red dragon of the book of Revelation, when the Spirit prompted him to move them on.

The thing to do is to be thorough. I recall a young person coming into the Lighthouse in Woking once and confiding in us that he had "a slight problem with a drug." The moment he said the words, I thought to myself, he will get nowhere with that attitude.

I didn't see him again myself. Hopefully, his was a timid way of introducing himself and he came back for more and was seen by others, being willing to confess his addiction as sin, something like this.

"Lord God, you have said that the most important thing is for us to love you and then love our neighbour as ourselves. I confess that I have done the opposite in focusing on myself with these drugs. Please forgive me; I turn from my selfishness utterly," or something along those lines. Then progress would be much more likely.

I found there was a lot to learn in deliverance ministry as it is sometimes called. In the end I decided it was like weeding the garden. Some weeds come out very easily. Others are entrenched, or have tap roots requiring a lot of digging. I'm told the roots of Japanese Knot Weed can grow up to eighteen inches a day. Bad news.

As a young person, I enjoyed *The Little Prince* by the French author Antoine de Saint-Exupery. One of the illustrations that impressed me was of a tiny planet which was so overwhelmed by baobab trees that the planet itself beneath them was hardly visible. The planet was more tree than rock.

What a state of affairs. The thing to do is not to make peace with the weeds in our lives but be determined with them if we want a fine garden.

And what a splendid tool scripture can be when used in this way.

Pastor Bob whom I wrote about earlier once told me that his job in his church was to keep the peace between two groups of believers. The first group were ones who were set free from their addictions instantly, following prayer, while the second group experienced a terrific struggle to get free which lasted ages. The first lot looked down on the others, asking them, where is your faith? The second lot were inclined to envy the first. Bob found himself in the middle trying to hold things together.

Note that they all got free, one way or another. As Bishop David Pytches once said at New Wine Christian Conference, "You just have to go with what God is doing. Some people are healed instantly. Others have to come back week after week. Others again, you pray with them on a Sunday evening and nothing appears to happen and then on Thursday, bing, they are healed, for no apparent reason. Just go with what God is doing."

I have never seen instant physical healing in answer to my prayers, to my knowledge, but I refuse to be discouraged and give up praying with people, because Jesus told the twelve to heal the sick and cast out demons, and so we are to do the same, and not worry about the results. Also, I seldom meet people I have prayed for a second time, so how would I know if they are healed or not.

There is such a lot to say on this subject, but what I want to point out is that we are now in the territory of delivering people from hell, which we discussed earlier. This is confirmed by the remark Phil made when all our praying was concluded, and he had thrown five full dustbin liners of unhealthy printed material out of his flat. "It was like coming up out of a big pit," he told me.

Now I doubt that he knew that Psalm forty begins "I waited and waited for the Lord. He bent down to me and heard my cry, and lifted me up out of the roaring pit and the miry mud and set my feet upon a rock, establishing my steps, and put a new song of praise to our God in my mouth. Many will see and fear and put their trust in the Lord..."

What's more, Psalm forty continues with the words 'sacrifice you did not desire... my desire is to do your will'. This might seem odd

– didn't God require elaborate sacrifices in his instructions given while the Israelites were at Mount Sinai and in the desert?

In the light of our enquiry, we can see that what Jesus wants is for the captives to be set free. Gatherings of believers offering praise is not the same as doing the will of our Lord, of plundering hell.

Why have you focused on casting out demons? It seems specialist to me.

For two reasons. Firstly, how are you going to get people out of hell if you neglect getting hell out of people?

Secondly, as I pointed out earlier, success in deliverance is the one thing we know about the mission of the seventy, so you could say that this being Jesus' widest circle of disciples, deliverance from evil spirits is for beginners rather than experts.

Note where we are with this matter. Apart from the church I led, none of the twenty-three other churches I belonged to ever mentioned demonisation and the freedom from it we have in Christ. During the last thirty years, I'm aware of just one meeting in Woking on the subject, given to a dozen of us. It was a joy to be present, even though the subject was only presented briefly. So much better than nothing at all.

It is therefore hardly surprising that people struggling with horrible things dominating their lives which are out of their control do not come forward to us for help. They would rather take their chance with under-funded agencies with long waiting lists that ultimately fail to deliver. We have really let our fellow human beings down badly by neglecting the deliverance that Jesus offers, abandoning them in their time of need. Let's see what we can do to remedy the situation by making our churches the go-to places for deliverance.

Oh dear, I am so sorry. Do you see how easily and quickly I fall back into the thinking I have grown up with, that the church is a building that I attend on Sunday mornings? It's going to be incredibly hard to reshape church life as being a group of believers working together to be Jesus in the community. If your response to this book is that maybe I do have a few good points that are worth making and we need to do some adjustments to our existing churches here and there then you have missed the point. We need to own up to what a mess we have made of it and humbly ask our Lord how to go forward from here. Big changes are called for.

Did you notice how most of my examples of best practice were taken from many years ago? What happened to my early zeal? Well, it got watered down by so-called church life. Jesus said to the grammarians and Pharisees, "you cross sea and land to make a proselyte, and when you succeed you make him doubly much a son of hell as you are." I'm afraid that describes what's become of me to a tee. God have mercy on me. The deadening effect of attending hundreds of worship services on my Christian life has not been good.

Returning to setting people free, when the occasion arises for prayer for deliverance these days, I introduce the person to the ideas from Graham Powell's book, claiming the promises we have in scripture, and invite them to order the nasty thing to leave themselves. Then hopefully they can carry on the process at home. I'm also careful to make sure that we have agreement on any prayer we are going to pray before embarking on it, as I have heard several stories of people who felt unhappy with prayers said over them by others to which they had not consented. So I check things out in advance before praying. Let's work as a team, deliverer and deliveree.

I have some further examples of using the Bible as a tool box.

In the mid nineteenth century, George Muller was very upset by all the orphans in Bristol, the city where he lived, but he had no resources to help. Then one day he noticed in Psalm sixty-eight that God is described as 'father of the fatherless'. He seized on this verse. No father would leave his children uncared for and unfed, he reckoned, especially not our loving heavenly father, so he began taking orphans in off the streets even though he had nothing to give them, relying on God to meet everyone's needs.

It was remarkable how food, money and help flowed in. Before long he had twenty children, and soon afterwards he needed to expand his premises as his faith grew. To cut a long story short, he ended up housing two thousand orphans in four large institutions, all without ever appealing for funds.

When he died, the people of Bristol lined the streets to honour him. Community leaders were moved too, and it seems that the social care we have for each other which developed over the course of the twentieth century can be traced back to him. And the buildings on Ashley Down? They became the University of the West of England in due course, in Muller Road, Bristol, where they can still be seen.

All this from seizing on a verse and making it his own.

We can do the same. My favourite verse for using like this is in Paul's first letter to the Thessalonians, chapter five. "Give thanks in everything, for that is the will of God in Jesus Christ for you."

I had to act on this after my five emergency stomach operations in 2018, none of which I was expected to survive, which left me so weak in the intensive care unit that the best I could hope for was a motorised wheelchair. It took a struggle, but eventually I was able to pray, thank you Jesus for this state I'm in, because if this is the path you want for me, I don't want to be anywhere else.

As it happens, I went on to make a full recovery to the astonishment of the medics. But that is not the point. I can't control my circumstances, but I can control my attitude. It was a Bible verse that taught me to do this, to be thankful even for difficulties and pain, since God has allowed them.

My hero, if you'll excuse the old-fashioned notion, is a lady I heard about but never met, who was told that her cancer was so bad that she would have to go into the terminal ward. It sounds awful.

"Oh good," she replied, "because there will be people in there who are depressed and broken, and I will be able to show them love and kindness."

I love that. You can't defeat a person with that attitude.

The thing is to keep an eye open for your own verses in the Bible, as Graham Powell suggests in his book, which is a splendid read by the way. It's one of my top books.

Twelve – Final Thoughts

A picture of a church plundering hell and populating heaven has been emerging as we have proceeded. I imagine such a church was there in the beginning, but generations of believers have allowed themselves to wander off like sheep to the point where today's churches are unrecognisably different, as we discussed earlier. So the key thing in church life seems to be not to allow ourselves to be distracted from Jesus and his stated will.

A mistake that is so easy to make is to be doing good things rather than doing God's things. That has been the theme of this book.

One particular distraction to my mind is unhelpful theology. I have a friend whose zeal for the Lord is off the scale. He prints tracts by tens of thousands and talks about the Lord to whoever he meets. Wonderful. However, because he believes in dispensations, whatever they may be, he insisted to me that healing is not for today and said I should stop.

Indeed, I ought to repent of speaking in tongues, I was told, and when I demurred he said I had the sin of pride.

My response is to ask whether his doctrine of dispensations is from the Lord whom I read about in the gospels, or from somewhere or someone else.

I think it is important to take the Bible text as it stands, and not look at it through our own pair of spectacles. When Saul saw the light, he was blinded for three days. Then Ananias came and prayed for him, and something like scales fell from his eyes. He had been a very zealous Pharisee up to that point, but now his way of looking at things had to change. He needed clear vision.

I attempt to take the Bible text at its face value, adding nothing and subtracting nothing; I hope you feel I have done that in this book. I think it is important if we are to serve our Lord fully.

Oughtn't we to do what the apostles and the early church did?

This sounds an excellent idea on first hearing, but if you examine it carefully, it's a departure, however slight, from what Jesus told us to do. He did not ask us to copy the twelve but to obey his instructions. They may have been doing that one hundred percent, of course, in which case it would make no difference, but they may not have been so thorough in their obedience.

It's worth noting that the twelve did not have a good track record in the four gospels. They were slow to grasp what was really going on – their hearts seemed to be hardened, as Jesus put it. Then early in the Book of Acts their concern was when God was going to establish the people of Israel; was this the time? That's a marked contrast with Jesus' desire to do the will of his father until he had finished his work, which we discussed earlier.

Later on, the disciples took a lot of persuading that the gospel was for gentiles as well as Jews. Finally, they went in for choosing a twelfth apostle to replace Judas Iscariot by casting lots, and with the exception of the Sisters of Loreto, from whose ranks Mother Teresa of Calcutta came and who use lot-taking in their decision process I believe, few of us would want to decide things by lot today. Who said there had to be a twelfth person added to the eleven anyway?

Ah, but the lot taking was before the Holy Spirit came.

So what you actually mean is we should copy the apostles post-Pentecost. The same caveat applies. Where their practice was what Jesus asked them to do, we will end up copying them by following the instructions of Jesus. Where it wasn't, we do well not to copy them.

Take the example of holding all things in common that the early believers adopted. Did Jesus ask his followers to do that? No, he did not. In fact he instructed something a great deal harder, which was to part with their possessions altogether. We are not called to copy them but rather to follow him.

Shouldn't we do what Jesus did?

This too sounds first class, and is generally produced as a clinching argument by someone who wants a particular line of action to be followed in a church setting. But there is a catch here. Few of us attempt to follow Jesus in every particular.

"Foxes have holes, and the birds of the air have nests, but the Son of Man has nowhere to lay his head," he once said. Are you going to give up your home and join the world of sofa surfers and rough sleepers in an attempt to copy Jesus? I thought not.

And what about his never speaking to people without a parable. Is that your style, you speakers? I've come across it just once in my experience when a friend of mine told an imaginative story without explanation to an assembly in a secondary school. It was a memorable talk that got them thinking. I've never witnessed it in seventy years of church services on Sunday mornings.

Thirdly, who among us has sought to walk on water in an attempt to copy the master? I once had to sit for long hours by the open air swimming pool in Wengen, Switzerland, where there are marks across the bottom of the pool which are the same as the signs used to mark the alpine paths in the area. I expect this was to show where the deep end began, but was the use of those particular markings the idea of some wag to encourage believers to step forth in faith to cross the pool, like Indiana Jones on his way to find the Holy Grail in the film about the last crusade, and find the water firm and supportive beneath them? Well, I never saw anybody make the attempt, either there or during many of my visits to the seaside in the UK.

So let's not hear any more about copying Jesus in an attempt to drum up support for an idea. We are called to obey him, not to copy him. Phew! That's a relief.

Paul said he copied Christ.

Yes, he did on one occasion. He was discussing the matter of food. He explained that he was seeking the good of many, so that they may be saved. He was not invoking a general principle.

Once again, although it sounds very godly, copying him is not what Jesus actually asked us to do. Most of it is beyond us, frankly. We are to follow his instructions, no more, no less.

And the way ahead?

In the well known parable, Jesus explained that the person who heard his words and acted upon them was building his house on rock, but the person who heard his words but did not act upon them was building his house on sand. I believe we have been doing the latter in our churches for many years. Don't be surprised if there's a crash sooner or later.

Personally, I would like to see all church buildings in our country that are designed for gathering together to worship God swept away, because I think that the witness for Jesus of Nazareth to our nation would be clearer without them than with them.

Some hope, and trying to enact this could itself be yet another distraction from getting on with the task before us.

The thing to do is to get started on doing church better. I envisage a small group, rather like the evangelism groups from Soho that we thought about, with the focus on action rather than discussion. The meetings should be more like the army briefings I recall from my school corps days – "D Company, you are to sweep the wood, and join up with F Company who have been entering the village from the river valley, quelling all resistance with small arms fire as you go" etc. Such meetings lead to action. Our churches suffer from all talk and no action to my mind.

God bless you as you try it, and thanks for reading.

Let's end with a recap of the key texts that we discussed earlier.

Paul explained to the Ephesians, "It is by grace we are saved, through faith, and this is not of yourselves; it is a gift of God, not of works, so that no person might boast. For we are his creation, created in Jesus Christ for good works which God has prepared in advance so that we might walk in them."

God has good works lined up for believers who put their faith in him.

Jesus described his church with the words "On this rock I will build my church, and the gates of Hades (hell) will not win a victory over it."

On departure, Jesus' final words were "'All authority in heaven and earth has been given to me. Going out, then, disciple all the nations, baptising them in the name of father, son and Holy Spirit, and teaching them to keep all I have commanded you and behold I am with you all days until the completion of the age."

Note the need to unearth what his commands were, by reading the gospels carefully. It's tempting for me to write here what I think the main ones are, but I think it's better that you should do the research yourself. All power to you as you do so.

I will just make one final point. Many of us think that the most important command of Jesus was that we are to love God with all our heart, soul and mind and our neighbour as ourselves, but actually this answer was given to the Pharisee who wanted to know the greatest commandments of the law. Jesus' own teaching about love was on a higher plane; we are to love our enemies.

One definition of enemies is people that threaten you most. A final story on this, and then I will stop. This book is proving hard to finish.

I was once asked to play the organ for a funeral of a lady whose life had been made hell by a number of young people that lived on her estate. She was actually in the process of assembling a rope and ladder to hang herself one morning when the phone rang. It was her niece, into whose head the idea had come, 'ring your aunt'.

"How are you, Aunt Mabel?"

The story came out with all its devastation.

"Why don't you come and stay with us for a bit?"

The visit was planned to be a fortnight long, but in the event it turned into fourteen years until Aunt Mabel died, not at the age of seventy as she had expected but aged eighty-four.

I have long loved that instance of the niece hearing from God and acting upon it, but now a new thought comes to me.

Is it out of the question that Aunt Mabel could have had a different attitude, one of thanking God for bringing these cruel young people into her life and asking him how she could win them for Christ, trying to engage with them despite their hostility and unkindness, and even going on one day to open the door to them, in great fear and trembling, and inviting them into her home and giving them hospitality, asking how they were getting on? In short, taking up her cross as the master called us to do, and not fearing the consequences.

Sounds dangerous? Well, please read *The Cross and the Switchblade* by David Wilkerson about his love for the street gangs in New York in the 1960s and Hebrews chapter eleven before giving your reply.

Think of the powerful witness to Christ such behaviour would have been.

There. That's it. The true Christian walk is a big challenge for all of us, but let's go to it.

Author's Note

My path has been a curious one. I left Christian ministry thirty-one years ago, and since then the churches I have been involved with have not wanted my input. I've become one of those who stand and sing and sit when instructed. This has given me time to reflect on the nature of our calling, leading to this book. I doubt that my insights would have been possible without me walking that path. Intriguing.

Further information about me can be gained from my website pennantpublishing.co.uk. Copies of this and my earlier books can be obtained from Amazon. If you felt able to leave a review online, even including a hostile one, I would be grateful. It would help us all. Thank you.

Index of Bible References

Zechariah 4:10 – don't despise the day

Matthew 4:18 – walking by the sea

Matthew 6:9 – Lord's prayer

Matthew 7:15 – wolves in sheep clothes

Matthew 7:24-27 – building on sand

Matthew 8:20 – foxes have holes

Matthew 9:36 – no shepherd for sheep

Matthew 10:1 – the twelve sent out

Matthew 10:8 – heal, deliver etc

Matthew 14:25 – walking on water

Matthew 16:18 & 18:15f – the church

Matthew 18:20 – Jesus with 2 or 3

Matthew 22:29 – Sadducees in error

Matthew 22:37-39 – love God and all

Matthew 23:15 – cross land and sea

Matthew 24:24 – false Christs will come

Matthew 26:17f – Passover meal

Matthew 26:41 – watch and pray

Matthew 28:20 – disciple all nations

Mark 1:15 – repent (not do penance)

Mark 4:34 – always a parable

Mark 8:17 – hearts hardened

Mark 9:29 – prayer for deliverance

Mark 11:22-3 – faith moves mountains

Mark 14:26 – hymn-sung

Luke 4:16 – Jesus' synagogue custom

Luke 10:1 – seventy sent out in pairs

Luke 10:17 – the seventy thrilled

Luke 18:1-8 – unjust judge

Luke 24:27 – Jesus explains prophecies

John 4:23 – worship in spirit and truth

John 4:34 – Jesus' meat and drink

John 5:19 – what is the father doing?

John 10:10 – thief kills steals & destroys

John 19:28 – I thirst

Acts 1:6 – is this the time?

Acts 1:14 – prayer together by 120

Acts 1:26 – casting lots

Acts 5:1-11 – Ananias and Sapphira

Acts 9:18 – scales fell from Paul's eyes

Acts 11:1-18 – gospel for gentiles also

Acts 12:5 – united prayer for Peter

Acts 13:1-3 – worshipping and fasting

Acts 20:29 – wolves in sheep clothes

Romans 3:23 & 6:23 – all sin and die

1 Corinthians 2:16 – the mind of Christ

1 Corinthians 6:19 – my body a temple

1 Corinthians 11:1 – Paul copies Christ

1 Corinthians 11:17f – Lord's supper

1 Corinthians 11:25 – as often as...

1 Corinthians 14:29 – weigh prophecies

2 Corinthians 5:19-21 – saved by Jesus

Galatians 5:22-23 – fruits of the Spirit

Ephesians 2:8-10 – saved by grace

Ephesians 5:19 – singing

Ephesians 6:10f – the believer's armour

Philippians 3:13-14 – Paul pressing on

Colossians 3:16 – singing

Colossians 4:6 – study how to talk

1 Thessalonians 5:18 – give thanks

1 Timothy 2:2 – pray for the king

Hebrews 10:24-25 – paroxysm of love

James 3:1 – teachers judged more

1 Peter 5:3 – little tin gods

1 John 1:9 – blood of Jesus cleanses us

1 John 5:3 – Love of God = obedience

Revelation 12:3 – a great red dragon

Books

J. B. Phillips, *The New Testament in Modern English*, Geoffrey Bles, London, 1960.

John Pollock, *Moody Without Sankey,* Hodder, 1983 for the anecdote about doing evangelism badly.

Graham and Shirley Powell, *Christian Set Yourself Free*, New Wine Press, 1983.

A. T. Pierson, *George Muller of Bristol*, Pickering and Inglis, London, 1972. Psalm 68:5 is quoted in chapter ten on page 141.

Antoine de Saint-Exupery, *The Little Prince*, translation by Katharine Woods, Heinemann, London, 1945. The illustration comes on page 18 of a recent edition by Collins.

David Wilkerson, *The Cross and the Switchblade*, Baker Books, 1984.

Printed in Great Britain
by Amazon

51547691R00088